Skywoman

Skywoman

LEGENDS OF THE IROQUOIS

Joanne Shenandoah-Tekalihwa: khwa
&
Douglas M. George-Kanentiio

ILLUSTRATED BY
John Kahionhes Fadden
&
David Kanietakeron Fadden

CLEAR LIGHT PUBLISHERS
SANTA FE, NEW MEXICO

Clear Light Publishers, 823 Don Diego, Santa Fe, NM 87501
WEB: www.clearlightbooks.com

First Edition
10 9 8 7 6 5 4 3 2 1

Library of Congress Cataloging-in-Publication Data

Shenandoah, Joanne
    Skywoman : legends of the Iroquois / Joanne Shenandoah, Douglas M. George ;
illustrated by John Kahionhes Fadden and David Kanietakeron Fadden.
        p.   cm.
    ISBN 0-940666-99-5
    1. Iroquois Indians—Folklore. 2. Iroquois mythology. 3. Legends—New York (State)
I. George, Douglas M. II. Kahionhes. III. Title.
    E99.I7S448   1996
    398.2'089975—dc20   96-32488
                                                          CIP

Contents

Skywoman

Before the beginning of time there lived humanlike beings in a place the Haudenosaunee call Skyworld. These were magical beings who were surrounded by a gentle light. They knew neither pain or death, nor were they ever ill. Earth years were but mere seconds to the Sky People. Yet they were similar to human beings and shared some qualities such as the ability to love and care for each other. They were like human beings in another way: they had the ability to dream.

One of the Sky People was a young woman named Iotsitsisen (pronounced Yo-ji-ji-sen) which means "Mature Flower." She was much loved by her parents and grew to be a beautiful and kind young woman. One day, however, Iotsitsisen experienced something no other Sky Person had ever felt: she became sick with a mysterious disease. Her illness caused her parents great concern because such a thing had never happened before and they had no idea how to make their daughter well again.

As hard as he tried, her father could not think of a way to make her well. One night, as he lay exhausted from worry, he had a magical dream. In his dream a spirit told him to take his daughter to a certain village where he would find a man called Taronhiawakon (De-lun-ya-wa-gon) or the "Holder of Heavens." This man would have the power to cure Iotsitsisen's sickness.

When Iotsitsisen was brought to Taronhiawakon, he immediately fell in love with the young woman and asked her father if he could marry her. Iotsitsisen's father agreed, provided Taronhiawakon could heal her. Calling upon the most powerful forces of the Skyworld, the young man was able to restore Iotsitsisen to good health. During their time together she became pregnant with his child.

His wife was once again in good health, and Taronhiawakon was happy to learn he was to be a father. But one night soon after that he had a disturbing dream. He was told by a spirit in the dream that his wife was to leave their home and enter a new world. They would find the way into this world beneath the roots of the Great Tree of Light, which stood in the middle of their village. The spirit told Taronhiawkon that Iotsitsisen's recent sickness meant she would have to leave Skyworld that very day.

Taronhiawakon awakened and went to the Great Tree, which grew so tall no one could see its peak. Taronhiawakon used his great strength to reach beneath its roots. Grasping the roots in his hands, he braced his legs. Then with a mighty push he toppled the Tree onto its side. Beneath it he discovered a large black hole exactly as his dream had foretold. He was afraid to put Iotsitsisen into this blackness, but he knew if he ignored the dream he would bring great troubles to the Sky People. Taronhiawakon returned home to get Iotsitsisen. His heart was heavy with sadness as he gently placed her into the black hole. He spoke to Iotsitsisen softly, promising to protect her by giving her a beam of light to guide her while he watched over her from the Skyworld.

Iotsitsisen felt only sorrow as she looked back at her husband. In the next instant she was carried away on a beam of pure light. When she looked down she saw a dark world covered with a deep and endless sea. Iotsitsisen wondered what would happen to her when she struck the water. She was afraid for her unborn child.

There was abundant life in this new world of water. Birds flew across its surface, water mammals floated above the waves, fish swam beneath it. However, none of these animals had ever seen such light as the one which was bringing Iotsitsisen to their world. In those days the animals would meet in council to discuss their concerns. They knew Iotsitsisen's coming was of interest to everyone, so a grand council of all the animals was called.

There was some argument as to who Iotsitsisen was and what her coming meant. The animals realized she did not have feathers, scales, fur, or webbed feet and all agreed it was important to prevent her from falling into the sea. The large and powerful geese flew to Iotsitsisen, who was falling slowly to earth, and made a place for her to stand by joining their wings together.

The other animals knew that the geese, however strong, could not hold up this new being for very long. From the depths of the sea came the great snapping turtle. Turtle said far beneath the sea was something called mud, which he would be willing to have placed on his back to make a place for Iotsitsisen to walk.

While Turtle could reach the bottom, he could not grasp the mud with his stubby legs.

Three animals said they would try to bring some mud to the surface. Beaver, Otter, and Muskrat all had paws which could grasp the mud. First to try was Beaver. He took a mighty breath and using his strong tail dove deep into the ocean. The animals waited for a long time. At last they saw the body of Beaver float to the surface. He had drowned before he could reach the bottom.

Second to try was Otter. He also took a deep breath and with his powerful whip of a tail went straight down into the sea. He was gone for a very long time before he too drifted back, lifeless and without the precious mud.

All hopes rested on Muskrat, a clever animal but without the strength of either Beaver or Otter. Yet he was determined to try. Filling his lungs with air, he disappeared under the waves. It seemed as though the animals waited for twice as long as they had for Otter. Finally, one of them noticed a small brown body rising from the deep. It was Muskrat. He was dead, but in his small paws was a tiny bit of mud. It was enough.

The animals carefully patted the mud upon
Turtle's shell while the geese gently placed
Iotsitsisen on his back. She walked about singing
a beautiful song while dancing on the mud.
Slowly, as if by the most wonderful magic, the
mud grew and grew until it stretched beyond
sight in all directions. Iotsitsisen thought about
what to call this new land and decided it should
be known as Turtle Island in honor of the
animal upon whom it rested.

In time Iotsitsisen gave birth to a daughter
she called Tekawerahkwa (De-ga-we-lah-gwa).
Iotsitsisen was as happy as she could be on Turtle
Island. But every now and then she would lift
her eyes to gaze towards her sky home, as if
searching for her parents and her husband,
the Holder of Heavens.

Grandmother Moon

Iotsitsisen (Yo-ji-ji-sen), "Mature Flower" the Skywoman, had come from her home above the heavens on a beam of light. She was placed by the geese on the back of the turtle. Using a small bit of mud from the bottom of the endless sea she sang and danced until a great land had been created that she called Turtle Island. It was then she gave birth to the child of the Holder of Heavens, a daughter she called Tekawerahkwa (De-ga-we-lah-gwa) or "Gusts of Wind."

Tekawerahkwa was a healthy child, full of energy and always ready to run and play. She roamed far and wide to explore everything and examine every animal. She loved to sing with the birds, swim alongside the fishes, and tease her otter friends by tugging on their long tails. But when she listened to her mother's stories of Skyworld, with all of its people doing the things people do, Tekawerahkwa became very sad.

This wonderful young girl had no playmate who was like her. She loved her mother deeply but could not help wishing for someone she could have as a friend. As the years passed, Tekawerahkwa grew to become a beautiful woman gifted with a singing voice so wonderful it caused the stars to twinkle.

A powerful being called West Wind was on one of his long journeys across the earth when he heard Tekawerahkwa singing. West Wind raced towards her so quickly he caused great waves to crash upon the land. The instant he saw Tekawerahkwa he fell in love; he had to have the young woman as his bride. He vowed he would watch over her from his place above the earth until he felt brave enough to ask Tekawerahkwa to be his wife.

After one busy day of exploring, Tekawerahkwa lay down to rest. As she lay sleeping West Wind crept beside her and upon her stomach he placed two arrows, one of which was tipped with white flint while the other was made of maple. Tekawerahkwa arose from her sleep to return home. Over the next few weeks her body began to change. Her mother saw the signs and knew her daughter was pregnant. She was happy about this since it meant she would be a grandmother.

Tekawerahkwa was carrying twins inside of her. These were most unusual beings because they could speak to one another. They were both males but very different. One had a skin as hard as flint marked by a sharp comb-like ridge upon his head. He was named Tawiskaron (Da-wis-ga-lon), "Ice Skin," and was fond of arguing with his brother. His twin, soft skinned and patient, was called Okwiraseh (O-gwi-la-seh) or "New Tree."

Tawiskaron said he had much to do in the world and would not wait to leave his mother in the natural way. He told Okwiraseh he would use the sharp comb on his head to cut his way through his mother's body until he reached her armpit; this was how he would be born.

Okwiraseh warned him against this, saying such an act would surely kill their mother. Tawiskaron ignored his brother and began to force his way through her while Okwiraseh was being born the natural way. Tawiskaron's stubborness cost Tekawerahkwa her life.

Iotsitsisen heard her daughter's birthing cries. She rushed to help Tekawerahkwa only to find her lifeless.

In a terrible rage she stood before her grandsons and demanded to know which one of them caused her death. Tawiskaron pointed to his brother and said it was Okwiraseh who had done the evil deed. Iotsitsisen grasped hold of Okwiraseh and flung him far away, believing starvation and cold would rid her of the murderous child.

Okwiraseh did not die. His grandfather Taronhiawakon was watching the child and came to his aid. In time he would teach Okwiraseh all he would need to know about surviving on the earth and then set him to work making the land a place of beauty.

The death of Tekawerahkwa would not be in vain. Iotsitsisen placed her head in the nighttime sky where it would forever watch over her earthly home. Because of her love of the earth she would be called the grandmother and be given the power over all waters. From her body grew corn, beans, and squash, plants which would one day feed millions of people.

The Twins

Okwiraseh (O-gwi-la-seh) was lonely.

He was sad that his mother Tekawerakwa (De-ga-we-la-gwa) "Gusts of Wind" had died giving birth to him and his twin brother Tawiskaron (Da-wis-ga-lon) "Ice Skin." Tawiskaron lied to his grandmother Iotsitsisen (Yo-ji-ji-sen) "Mature Flower," blaming Okwiraseh for their mother's death. The grandmother believed Tawiskeron and cast his brother away.

The years passed and Okwiraseh grew into a young man. He wandered aimlessly on Turtle Island until one day he came to the edge of a lake. Seeing a world reflected in the water, he dove beneath its surface to find out if indeed there was another world similar to his own on the other side.

Beneath the waters Okwiraseh found himself in a new land. He walked about for some time until he noticed smoke coming from a lodge in the distance. As he approached the lodge he saw a man sitting before its entrance. The man invited Okwiraseh into his home.

The man said he had been watching Okwiraseh on the other side of the water and was concerned about the manner in which Iotsitsisen was treating her grandson. His name was Taronhiawakon (Da-lon-ya-wa-gon) "Holder of Heavens." The grandfather of Tawiskaron and Okwiraseh, he had guided his grandson to his own lodge to teach him how to bring beauty into the world.

For many days Okwiraseh sat before Taronhiawakon, listening patiently as the older man gave him his instructions. He was told he would create new animals, fishes, and birds, but the most important task was the forming of human beings from the mud of the earth.

Okwiraseh returned from the water world to begin his great work. He dug channels for the rivers to flow, raised mountains and planted trees. He taught the birds to sing and the water animals to dance. He made rainbows and soft rains from which the earth quenched her thirst.

Not all was peaceful on the land, however. Tawiskaron, his evil twin, watched what his brother was doing and became envious. He followed Okwiraseh and for every good thing he made, Tawiskaron would create its opposite.

Instead of smoothly flowing rivers Tawiskaron made dangerous rapids; he replaced the cleansing winds with destructive hurricanes and powerful tornadoes. When Okwiraseh planted medicinal plants to cure illness, Tawiskaron made poisonous roots and deadly berries.

After laboring for many years Okwiraseh rested to examine his work. He was pleased with the things he had done. Tawiskaron was not pleased with his creations. He had watched his brother make the world a beautiful place and was very angry because he could not master the skill of making living things except for bats, snakes, and lizards.

While Okwiraseh was far away creating ever more wonderful things, Tawiskaron

decided to steal all the animals and place them in a large cave deep inside a mountain. He then blocked the entrance to the cave with boulders to prevent them from escaping.

Okwiraseh returned home only to discover that his creatures had disappeared. His cries of grief were heard by a tiny mouse who, moved by Okwiraseh's sadness, told him what his brother had done and where the animals were being hidden.

Hastening to the entrance of the cave, Okwiraseh used his magic to shake the mountain, causing a wide split from which the animals emerged. Tawiskaron heard the rumbling from his home deep inside the mountain; he sped to the cave's mouth and saw most of the animals escaping. Some were too large to fit through the hole and these Tawiskaron forced back into the cave before once again sealing the entrance with an avalanche of rocks.

Okwiraseh was very angry with his brother. He decided to confront Tawiskaron through a game to decide which brother would rule the day and which would control the night. Tawiskaron accepted the challenge. The brothers would play a game using half

white and half black stones shaken and tossed in a
large bowl. The winner would be the one who threw
a certain combination of black and white stones.
He would rule the day and the loser would be banished
into the darkness.

Iotsitsisen, the grandmother, was told of the game
by Tawiskaron, her favorite grandson. She decided she
would give Tawiskaron secret power to control how the
stones would fall.

Knowing his grandmother would use her powers
to help Tawiskaron, Okwiraseh decided to play a trick
on both of them. He called the small chickadees and
painted their heads white on one side and black on the
other. As he sat down to play he was able to toss them
far into the sky and command them to fall as he wished.

Tawiskaron lost the game and resented his brother
even more than before. Slyly, Tawiskaron asked
Okwiraseh what thing on the earth could cause
him deadly harm. Okwiraseh had been told by his
grandfather that his brother would ask this question.
Okwiraseh told his brother he was afraid of the
cattail weed, for it would cause him to bleed if he
were struck by it.

Okwiraseh in turn asked his brother what thing might cause him pain. Tawiskaron said it was the antlers of the deer and flint shards, which would break off his hard skin if they stuck it.

As they spoke Okwiraseh was stoking a large fire. Tawiskaron protested, for the heat was causing his flint skin to crack. Okwiraseh placed even more wood into the flames. Tawiskaron grew so angry he left to find a cattail to strike his brother. He returned to beat Okwiraseh. The two tumbled on the ground, hitting each other with powerful blows.

As they tumbled, Okwiraseh found a deer antler. He grabbed the antler and hit his brother with it. Great yellow sparks flew from Tawiskaron as chips fell from his body. The brothers battled for many days across the land, uprooting trees, gouging out large patches of earth, and pushing aside mountains, lakes, and rivers.

The fight finally ended with Okwiraseh the winner. He banished Tawiskaron to live in caves far beneath the earth where he lives to the present day, waiting for his chance to return to the world of light.

The Star Dancers

A long time ago the Iroquois peoples left their homes in the dry southwestern lands of Turtle Island to search for a place to plant their crops and raise their families. After many generations of wandering they settled along the waters of what is now New York State. Their new homes were in a beautiful land marked by gently rolling hills, fertile valleys, and deep, clear lakes.

They were pleased with the great forests of white pines and broad-leafed elms. The wood carvers and builders among them found that these trees made fine homes once they were cut and cleared of branches.

Before they began their work, however, the builders thought carefully about what type of dwelling would be best suited to the region. They came up with a building that was comfortable, easy to construct, and large enough to hold many families. It was to be called a "longhouse" and in time would symbolize all the Iroquois tribes.

The People of the Longhouse became wealthy in their new land. They cleared large parts of the forest so they could plant their crops of corn, beans, and squash. Their luck was good as year followed year of bountiful harvests.

After some years they began to take their fortune for granted. They forgot the ancient ceremonies of thanksgiving the Creator had taught them. They became jealous of each other and began to quarrel and fight. Their villages split apart into opposing groups with some leaving their homes because they were afraid.

The children suffered most from the hurtful ways of their parents. Instead of awakening in the morning and rushing out to play with their friends, the children were told not to speak with anyone who was not a part of the family, nor were they to stray far from the longhouse. If they disobeyed, the parents cut thin willow branches to whip them on their legs and backs. Many times children were sent to bed without dinner.

In one village lived a group of seven young boys and girls. They had heard stories from their grandparents about the old days, when the People were happier because everyone shared stories, songs, and the fruits of their work. They listened carefully as the older people spoke about the ancient ceremonies when they used to sing, dance, and hold great feasts to honor Mother Earth. They were also told of a time when children were treated as blessings from the Creator and were never hurt by their parents.

The group decided they would sneak away from their longhouses and meet together in a secret place far into the woods. Each one of them would bring a bit of food to share with the others. During one of these gatherings they decided to bring back the old ways and hold their own ceremonies.

The children chose one of the boys among them to be the guardian of the ceremonies. His name was Broken Ice; he would now be called a "faithkeeper" and would have the task of speaking for the entire group. Since this was a serious responsibility, Broken Ice felt he needed someone to work with him. The group agreed and chose Bright Day, a young girl, to be the second faithkeeper.

Holding a thanksgiving ceremony is not a simple thing. The children would have to learn many songs

and sacred dances, as well as preparing the right foods. They would also have to know the exact words of prayer so their efforts would be accepted by the Creator. The preparations took many weeks.

With each passing day the children had to be ever more cautious about leaving their homes. The youngest among them, a small boy named Gathering Wind, found it very hard to think up reasons for defying his parents. He would lie awake on his sleeping platform late into the night worrying about being caught as he tried to slip away. He loved his mother and father, who, unlike the other parents, showed their child much kindness and love. But he also felt his friends were doing something very important and was happy they trusted him with so wonderful a secret.

Gathering Wind was very good at crawling into the storage sheds to get food for the group. He could be as still as a mouse until everyone was gone, then he would stuff as much as he could in his leather pouch before sneaking away.

Not all went as well as the children would have liked. A few times some of them were caught leaving the village and were whipped severely. The others would huddle together, listening with fear as their friends cried out in pain and sorrow.

The parents of the children realized something strange was taking place. They punished the children harshly. Besides the whippings, they were not given food and were kept inside the longhouses and tied to their beds.

Gathering Wind found his way to where the punished children were. He brought them corn mush and maple sugar to eat and medicine for their wounds. He told them funny stories to raise their spirits. Life became harder for these children, but they vowed they would not stop meeting with their friends.

One day, when all seven children managed to find their way to the secret place, Bright Day told them of a story she had heard from her grandmother about a special place beyond the sky. Bright Day said this land was full of wonderful things and magical people who loved all children. Skyworld, she had been told, was the original homeland of the longhouse people. If the children could go there, they would be welcomed home by the ancestors of the first human beings.

The children thought about this story over the next

few days. They were almost ready to hold the great festival of thanksgiving, even though they had little to be grateful for. It was important, they thought, to believe there was something better than what they knew. If it was in Skyworld, maybe that was where they should go.

It was the evening before the day of the ceremony, when the children had planned to gather in their secret place to sing and dance as had not been done in many years. It was a difficult night for all of them, for it seemed their parents sensed something strange was about to take place. The beatings of that night were harder than ever but not one of the children spoke a word.

Finally, during the time just before dawn, the children crept from their homes. Each one was carrying a gift hidden to share with the others. They were as quiet as shadows. Not even the village dogs were awakened as they slipped by.

Being extra careful to disguise their tracks the children made their way to the secret place. Broken Ice was the first one there. He embraced each child as they entered the meeting grounds. When all were present he built a small fire in the clearing and took a handful of sacred tobacco from his pouch. One by one the children touched the tobacco. Broken Ice then began to place the tobacco into the fire as he spoke the Thanksgiving Prayer he had learned from his grandfather. His words came from deep inside him and seemed to rise with the smoke to the top of the trees and beyond.

The children thought carefully about Broken Ice's prayer. They seemed to come to a mysterious understanding of what they must do to escape from their painful lives. When Broken Ice finished, Bright Day asked the children to gather in a circle. The dance was about to begin. The children joined hands and began to chant in unison. Their song was one of sadness for their families and of a great longing for the Skyworld and the love of their ancestors.

The parents had noticed their children were missing and had begun to search for them in the forest. They shouted for them to come home and threatened great punishments if the children did not come out from hiding. One of them noticed the smoke rising from the children's fire and called the others. Soon they would find the secret place.

The children did not hear their parents coming.

They were singing to the Creator with all of their hearts, giving thanks for being alive and asking Holder of Heavens to bring them to Skyworld. They danced as they sang, their feet clothed in ragged leather. Slowly, they began to rise from the ground, but they did not notice for they were looking up towards their original home. They sang and danced, rising ever higher, feeling the great joy of being the children of the sky.

Their parents heard the children's chants and watched with amazement and alarm as the children danced above the trees, then higher still as with each song. The parents cried out, first in anger then despair as the children went further into the sky. They heard the words of the songs and suddenly understood the harm they had caused the children.

Gathering Wind's parents felt more grief than the rest. They had truly cared for their son and had never struck him. His mother wept as she called for Gathering Wind to return home. He heard her calls as he ascended to the sky. Turning from the others he looked down to see his mother, tiny and far below kneeling on the ground, her arms raised to him.

Gathering Wind's dance faltered and he broke the

chant. As he stopped singing he began to fall even as the others continued to journey upwards. He gathered speed as he fell, rushing through the air back to his mother until he became a streak of burning light.

The dancers disappeared into the heavens leaving their families in sorrow. In their sadness they promised they would never again strike any child. Nor would they forget to be thankful to the Creator, a promise the People of the Longhouse renew whenever they see a falling star. The ancient ceremonies were brought back, as were the old songs and dances, which gave much joy to the People.

On clear evenings they would gather outside the longhouses to watch the sky. There, to the northeast, they saw a small cluster of stars where the dancers had faded into the night.

The Little People

There once was a young Seneca man named Snow who lived with his parents along the banks of a river in the land of the People of the Great Hill. He was a strong and vigorous young man who took great pleasure in exploring the hills, fishing in the river and hunting in the nearby forests. Snow was an excellent hunter because he had listened carefully as his elders taught him how to track animals, where to set his nets for fish, and what plants to eat while he was far from home.

A skilled and successful hunter, he gave the best part of his catch to the elderly and sick. He obeyed his parents in all things, even when they said he was never to venture towards the south, where strange creatures were said to dwell.

One day Snow awoke to find his family hungry and in need of food. It was early spring and many of the larger animals were just emerging from their deep sleep. Their thin bodies offered little in the way of food, so Snow decided he would bring down a few birds with his bow and arrow. He began to follow a small flock of

pigeons southward until they led him along a stream
into a deep gully. Soon, the walls of the gully rose
higher and higher and became ever more narrow
until Snow could barely see the sky above him and
he could not turn around.

Snow had barely enough room to sit down on a
large rock. He was sad and discouraged, knowing he
was completely lost and thinking he was very much
alone. Snow was in this black mood when he heard the
loud crack of a stone striking the rock upon which he
was sitting. He stood up alarmed, with his shoulders
brushing against the canyon walls. Another stone was
thrown at him, bouncing off his arm. Snow tried in vain
to turn around—only to be hit in the forehead. The
blow struck him so hard he was knocked senseless.
His body remained upright and in the firm grip of the
narrow canyon.

It was a long while before Snow slowly began to
awaken from a dark, deep sleep. Although he was in
great pain from the wound caused by the stone, he was
glad he could still move. He heard many voices about
him but decided to keep his eyes closed until he could
figure out who had struck him. He was lying down on a
soft bed of furs; by carefully moving his hands about his

body, he realized his head had been bandaged. Snow was relieved he had not been tied up. As the throbbing in his forehead lessened, he became curious to know more about the people who had brought him to this strange place.

Snow heard footsteps around him, as light as those of a small child. He could also hear the beating of a water drum and laughter, as if a group of people were having a good time. He understood what the people were saying and even recognized their songs. Satisfied that he was not in danger, Snow opened his eyes and sat upright.

Snow looked around the dwelling with awe, for he was in the lodge of a people who were fully grown yet the size of the smallest Iroquois child. They looked, dressed, walked, and talked like normal adults but stood no taller than his knees. He was sitting before a dancing fire and when the little people saw he was awake they greeted him with joy.

A chief of the little people approached Snow with his left hand raised high, his palm open. He asked Snow if he had tobacco. When the young man reached into his pouch to give him a handful the chief nodded with delight. He welcomed Snow into the home of the little people. He told Snow they had held a great council of all his kind during which it was decided to bring one of the big human beings there to receive a special teaching.

The little people were caretakers of the earth. They had special powers over flowers, fruits, and healing plants. They had watched as human beings had grown in numbers until they were now settled throughout the land. Over the years, however, the taller beings had forgotten some of their ancient ways and were beginning to ignore the instructions of the Creator.

As a result, Snow was told, there was much sickness among the people, along with disputes, quarreling, and fighting. The little people were afraid of the harm the human beings would bring to the earth, so they had selected Snow to carry their words and knowledge to all Native people.

Snow was given instruction in many things, such as how to release the healing power of the plants and which charms to use in hunting. He was told the little people had a great love for tobacco and would be very happy if the human beings would place the smoking leaves where they could find them.

Finally, after what seemed to be days full of learning,

Snow was taken by the chief to a clearing in the forest near his home. He was given many gifts. One of the presents from the chief was a secret charm made of a clear stone which gave Snow the great power to heal. Snow was sad to leave his small friends but also glad to return home to his parents.

As Snow approached his village he noticed things were different. The trees seemed larger, the longhouses older. The people he thought he knew were changed, and there were younger ones he did not remember at all. He saw two very old people sitting in front of his lodge. They were his parents. Snow was amazed to see they had aged many years while he was gone.

Overjoyed at his return, they said he was thought to have died long ago when he went hunting. Snow realized the few days he had spent with the little people were many years to human beings.

Snow did not forget his promise to teach his people all he had learned from his small friends. From that day forward he taught the songs, ceremonies, and rituals of the little people while reminding his own people always to be thankful to the Creator and to walk gently upon the earth, lessons the People of the Longhouse have never forgotten.

The Evergreens

When the Creator first walked about the Earth it was a place of tall, rock-strewn mountains, vast desolate plains, and empty seas. His great task was to make Earth a beautiful place by placing living things upon her body. He made the smallest of insects and the largest of animals; he placed birds in the sky and fish in the wide seas.

He scattered flowers about to give color to the land with grasses to brush against the winds. Some plants had roots which reached deep into the ground to grasp the soil firmly, while others grew on river bottoms or within swamps and marshes.

Trees of many kinds were also made, some tall and graceful, others short and stout. All trees were cloaked in the most wonderful green. Leaves and needles remained on their branches throughout the four seasons, coloring the earth with on-going life.

The Creator told each living thing how they were to exist upon the Earth; he warned that if they should break the rules which bound them to their particular ways, great troubles would result. For many generations harmony existed on Earth as each living being found comfort living in the way of its own family.

One day the Creator spoke to the living things. He said he had done his best to spread life on Earth and was well pleased with his labors. But, he said, he had to leave Earth to travel to other worlds where he would plant and spread life. He assured the living things he would return; to mark his promise he asked the trees to watch over Earth in his absence.

Be careful, he told the trees, not to fall asleep while I am away, because the Earth needs to be protected. He instructed the trees to remain ever alert even during the dark months. They were to use their green leaves to provide shelter for the animals and insects against the wind, rain, snow, and cold. The trees promised they would do their best and would not rest, not even for a moment.

Content that the Earth was safe, the Creator departed on his distant journeys. He was gone for a very long time yet the trees remained alert. Season followed season until the years flowed by beyond counting, but they did not waiver in their task until one fateful day.

A maple tree, standing proud among her kin, watched as winter approached. She noticed that many animals were storing away food in secret places so they would have nourishment when Earth was covered by deep snow. Others grew thick fur and searched for caves and deep crevices where they would sleep during the coldest moons.

Maple wondered at this strange thing called sleep. The animals would curl in a tight ball, close their eyes and begin to breathe very slowly. They did not awaken to eat or play or dance but seemed to enter a magical place somewhere deep in their minds.

Maple wanted to join them there for she missed their chatter as they scampered among her branches or ran around her trunk. She grew lonesome during the long, moonless nights waiting for the return of the Creator. She found his words difficult to recall; it had been so long since she heard his soothing voice or was warmed by his touch as he caressed her rough bark.

Perhaps, she thought, it might be possible to be with the Creator by turning away from the outside world and sleeping. Maple discovered it was a simple thing to do once she tried. She turned her leaves, of which she was very proud, inward while slowing her flow of sap and curling her roots into Earth. Soon, she became very quiet, barely rustling her leaves or moving her branches.

Other trees, particularly the broad leaves, found Maple's sleep most curious. No matter how hard they tried, they could not awaken her from this thing called sleep. Throughout the long winter, when the other trees shivered in the bitter cold, Maple seemed content and at peace during her slumber.

Finally, after many months, Earth began to turn once again to the Elder Brother the Sun. His bright daytime light heated ground, air, and water, and awakened the animals, who emerged from their burrows much thinner than in the fall and very hungry.

Maple also stirred, shuddered, and awoke. Her branches sprouted more leaves as she grew taller with the lengthening of days. The other trees with broad leaves were amazed at the change in Maple and vowed to try to sleep when the cold moons returned. They were so excited by this new thing they forgot their promise to the Creator, all except the slender trees with the needle-thin leaves. They refused to be tempted by

sleep even if it meant their branches would break under heavy snow and their tops would be bent by icy winds.

Winter could not come fast enough for the broad leaves. They followed Maple's example, turned their leaves, slowed the flow of sap and turned their thoughts inward. As the years passed many other trees joined them until it seemed only the thin-needled ones were left to watch Earth atop lonely mountains, across rocky hills, and on the thin soils where they alone grew.

Yet the Earth watchers did not give up.

Finally, the Creator returned to Earth from his visits to the other worlds. He saw what had happened to his trees, to whom he had entrusted Earth. He was most saddened by the failure of Maple and her friends to fulfill their duties, even as he was very proud of the thin-needled trees.

The Creator then made a decision: from that day onwards those trees who went into sleep would lose their precious leaves during winter. They would not be able to enjoy the clear, star-filled nights nor would they sing with the wind. They would have to grow new leaves every spring and wait many weeks before becoming fully dressed.

Those trees who stayed awake would from then on always be cloaked in green. They would bring eternal joy to Earth with their beauty and special songs. They would be called "evergreens" by all living things, a name of great honor since green is the color of life.

And so it is to this day. The evergreens remind us to be patient and always live by our promises. They continue to watch over the land, a task the Iroquois people have honored by selecting the eastern white pine as their symbol. Beneath the branches of this Great Tree of Peace all the Peoples of the Longhouse would one day come together to change their way of life and put an end to war.

How the Bear Clan Became Healers

Once, long ago, in an Indian village on the southern shores of beautiful Lake Ontario, there lived a people called the Iroquois. They had nine different families or clans named after animals the Iroquois felt were special. These clans were the Beaver, Wolf, Turtle, Snipe, Deer, Bear, Hawk, Eel, and the Heron.

Each clan lived in its own building called a "longhouse" because they were up to three hundred feet in length. Each clan had their own part of the village where clan members grew food such as corn, beans, and squash. But despite all their gifts from the Creator, the Iroquois had become selfish and greedy. When they became sick, they were so jealous and fearful they trusted no one to help them, as the gift of healing was unknown to them.

One day an elderly man arrived at the village. The man was bent with weariness, his face wrinkled and dirty, his clothes ragged, his moccasins torn. He was weak with hunger from his long journey.

As was the custom among the Iroquois he went to the first longhouse he saw. This building had a Beaver sign painted on it, so he knew the Beaver clan lived inside. Since the Iroquois believe all homes were owned by the women, he approached the oldest woman there and asked if she had any food to eat. She sent him away saying they had nothing to spare for a useless old man. He could see the house was full of drying corn and he smelled a rich stew cooking in a great pot hung over the fire.

The old man stumbled on to the longhouse of the Eel where he was pushed aside and simply ignored while they feasted on venison and fish. He then went to the Herons, where the entrance of the longhouse was blocked by a group of mean young men who called him terrible names. It seemed every family forgot the Creator's instructions to honor the elders and feed the hungry, for he was turned away by every clan.

Finally, just as he was about to faint with hunger, he noticed a small Bear clan longhouse at the edge of the village. A young woman was leaving the longhouse when she saw the old man. She immediately went up to him and brought him inside her home. The home was poor when compared with the longhouses of the other clans.

The young woman sat the old man next to the fire, in the seat of honor. She spoke gently to him as she washed his face and hair. She quickly prepared a warm meal of corn mush sweetened with strawberries and maple sugar. When she saw he was sleepy, she prepared a warm bed of soft furs. When he awakened the next morning she had sewn new buckskin clothes for him and repaired his moccasins.

The woman, called Little Light, spent many days with the old man, even asking him to teach her children. Little Light grew to love the old man for his gentleness and wisdom. It was therefore not surprising that she was alarmed when she found he had become ill during the night. He told her he had a stomach ache. The Iroquois had no cure since they had no knowledge to heal sickness. He told her there was a plant called ground ivy growing in a certain place. Before taking the herb, she was to make an offering of tobacco and say a prayer of thanks to the plant. Then, she was to bring the plant to the longhouse, where he would show her how to prepare a tea which would cure him of his sickness.

Little Light did exactly as she was told and was very happy when the old man got better. She called all

of the village together for a great feast to share her joy and tell how she helped heal the old man's illness.

Her happiness did not last long. The next day the old man could not rise from his bed because he had great pains in his head. He told the worried Little Light she was to go into the forest where she would find the beech tree at a special place. She was to take a piece of the tree's bark and leaves but not before making an offering of tobacco and thanking the tree for using its powers. She did exactly as she was told. She brought the bark home and, following the old man's instructions, prepared a potion for him to drink. He was swiftly cured.

Every day the old man was ill with a new sickness. One morning he complained of crippled hands, which she cured with chestnut leaves. When he lost his voice, she was instructed to prepare a tea from the inner bark of the chestnut. He had a fever, which she treated with the bark of the pussy willow. So it went, on and on, for many weeks. Each day Little Light followed his instructions, found the right plants, made an offering, gave thanks, and prepared the medicines as she was told. Little Light never complained, even when she was afraid the old man would never be well.

One day, as she was carrying yet another medicine plant for the old man, she noticed a bright light coming from within the longhouse. Fearing there was a fire, she rushed towards home. Just as she reached the door a young man surrounded by a beautiful, warm white glow stepped outside. Little Light shrank back in fear but he reached out, and in the gentlest words she had ever heard, spoke to her.

The young man said he was the Creator. He was concerned that human beings had forgotten his instructions for them to be kind, generous, and always to respect their elders. He said all people suffer sickness. He had provided a cure for every illness, but the Iroquois had become too greedy and mean to learn. He had come in the disguise of an old man to see which person had the goodness of heart to relieve suffering. He said all the clans but for the Bear had proven to be unworthy. Because of Little Light's generosity to a ragged old man the Creator would give all Bear clan members the power of healing. So it is from that day to this, because of the good heart of a young woman called Little Light, the Bear clan have been the healers for the Iroquois peoples.

The Creature from the Sea

Long ago, in the southwest part of Turtle Island, a small group of people became unhappy with the way things were. They lived in a dry land, where the sky seemed without end. They were required to labor many hours in their small fields of corn since rain was scarce and water hard to come by. Each day they would collect their small clay pots and walk a great distance to a shallow river, where they would gather muddy water for plants which always seemed to be thirsty. Since they were surrounded by enemies, they had to make their homes in hidden places far from the river.

Surely, their leaders thought, there must be a better place, a friendly land with rain and tall trees rather than stunted ones with limbs so bent it took many hours to cut them. In time, after many prayers had been said, one of the young women had an unusual dream. She said while in deep sleep she was taken by a large blue heron on a great journey, far to the northeast. The heron carried her on his back across a land of tall grass which fed buffalo herds whose numbers were beyond counting.

As they flew on they came to a large river which flowed from north to south, and as they followed its course upriver they came to a place where it was joined by two other rivers. Here there was a town where more people lived than she had ever imagined were on the earth. The heron did not stop there. Instead, it followed one of the rivers eastward for a long while, then entered a land of deep blue lakes which, the heron said, were made when the Creator scratched the earth.

In this place, she was told, her people would one day settle, build their homes, and raise their families. It was here, the heron said, they would increase in numbers and, after many generations had passed, become a powerful nation known throughout the world.

The people were convinced they must follow the young woman's dream if they were to survive. One special day they gathered their few belongings and began to walk to the east to find the great rivers and the land of deep lakes.

The journey took many generations to complete, but in the end the people found the hills and lakes they had been promised. They were pleased to find the soils

fertile and the forests and rivers full of game and fish. It was an exciting time to be wandering about and exploring the new land.

A boy named Carries the Fire took the greatest pleasure in seeing what was beyond the next bend of a river or over the next hill. He would return home with stories about stone giants, monstrous bears, and flying heads. Some of the stories the people believed to be true while others they thought came from his dreams.

Carries the Fire insisted all he had told them was true. He said he had met another people a few days paddle to the east. Through signs and pictures they told him the river he was traveling upon turned to the south before emptying into an endless salt sea. In this water, he was told, creatures dwelt who were of such size they could swallow ten men at one time. Again, his story was met with doubt, for no one could imagine their precious grains of salt filling an entire sea or beasts of such appetites as to eat an entire man without breaking him into pieces.

Carries the Fire was sad because no one seemed to believe him. He bade his family goodbye and set out to find the sea for himself. He was determined to bring back enough salt to prove he was right. If he was fortunate enough to catch one of the young sea creatures, he would bring it back to show his people.

Carries the Fire's journey was as he had been told: after many days of hard paddling, first to the east and then to the south, he noticed the waters were tasting of salt even as the banks of the river were becoming ever

farther apart. Soon afterwards he came to a large bay shielded by high cliffs to the west. He saw smoke arising from the lodges of a nearby village and decided to ask the people where he might trap a young creature.

Carries the Fire did as he was taught: before entering the village he made a small camp, lit his cooking fire, and put flame to the tobacco in his clay pipe. It was not long before his smoke was noticed and a man sent to inquire who he was. Since Carries the Fire was very young, the man believed he was no danger to the people, so he escorted the boy to the village.

Carries the Fire was given food, and a place for him to sleep was set aside in one of the lodges. The next day he was brought before a council of elders. Through signs he told them of his travels and his desire to see the endless lake of salt. They were clearly impressed that such a young boy had come so far. They agreed to give him as much salt as he could carry.

He then used signs to ask them if they knew of the creature large enough to swallow ten men whole. The elders told him through signs that such a creature did in fact exist and could be seen swimming in the salt water not too far from where they were.

When Carries the Fire signaled he wanted to capture a young creature to carry home, they looked at him with surprise. Such a thing would be most difficult since the mother creatures protected their young as fiercely as a bear protects her cubs. They would not catch a water creature for him. Carries the Fire was saddened by this. He feared he would be called a liar or a dreamer if he went home without the beast.

When food was brought before the council, Carries the Fire absently added corn to his bowl of fish stew. One of the elders wanted to know what the yellow food was, so Carries the Fire gave him a handful of corn. The boy was surprised when the elder's eyes widened in pleasure as he ate the corn. He thought all people ate as he did.

Carries the Fire was urged to share more corn. The elders became excited and the people of the village came running. Everyone was trying to grasp at least a few kernels and Carries the Fire had nothing left. The people wanted more.

It was then Carries the Fire had an idea how to get what he wanted. Carries the Fire told them he could get them as much corn as they wanted in his distant homeland if they would bring him a sea creature.

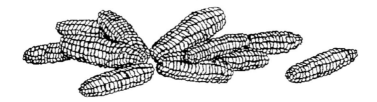

His request caused excitement among the salt water people. They withdrew to their council grounds to discuss Carries the Fire's offer. After some time they returned and signed to him they would send the strongest of their men to the sea, where they would try to capture a beast. The men were gone for many days. Finally, they were seen in the distance with something large swimming between their boats.

As they approached the shore, Carries the Fire saw they were pulling a huge water creature. It was a strange creature with small eyes and rough gray skin. It blew out gusts of moist air from a hole in the top of its large head.

As Carries the Fire prepared to leave the salt water people, he realized he could never hope to paddle upstream with his creature. The elders signed to him they would send six of their largest canoes with him to help with the creature if they could bring back as much corn as they could carry. To this Carries the Fire agreed.

The journey home took many days. His creature was a strong one for it was able to swim alongside the canoes tied with straps and rawhide ropes.

Carries the Fire's people were excited to have him back and more so when they saw the creature. They could tell it was an intelligent animal, hungry and tired. The salt water people were given corn and in return gave the river people salt and foods such as oysters with hard shells of bright purple and white. It was agreed before the salt water people left that trade between the peoples would begin.

Carries the Fire's people soon discovered that the sea beast had a huge appetite which demanded ever more quantities of fish. Within a short time they were forced to work harder to feed the creature, and their other duties began to be neglected.

The village elders met to discuss the problem. They told Carries the Fire the sea creature would have to find a home where it could feed itself, a place which resembled its own home. They knew of such a place, to the northeast, where there was a fresh water lake which was so large it seemed to curve into the sky. There, they said, the creature would have its freedom and could find its own food.

The elders decided the people would have to pull, push, and carry the sea creature through rivers, creeks,

and small lakes. It took many days to reach the great
lake. There the sea creature was released to the water
they called Sken-yet-de-li-yo or the "Beautiful Water"
(now called Lake Ontario).

It is said the sea creature lives there still, content to
dwell in caves at the bottom of the lake, shy of people
but ever remembering the boy called Carries the Fire.

Jikonsahseh,
Mother of Nations

On the western borders of the Iroquois lands, where the mighty Niagara Falls empties the waters of Lake Erie into placid Lake Ontario there dwelt a peaceful people known to all as the Neutral Nation. Despite their name, they were not quite as meek as one might think. Certainly, they were friendly, hospitable people but they were also sharp traders whose bartering skills brought them great wealth.

And they were clever politicians. They kept out of the fighting that was going on among other Iroquois nations by agreeing to keep their borders open and to supply all the war parties with food and materials.

The Neutrals were suspicious of everyone. Yet they were careful not to anger anyone they had cause to fear. They trusted no one. When Native people doubted the sincerity of a person they would say "He is as honest as a Neutral." "A Neutral," they would say, "is quick with a handshake—and even faster with his fingers."

There was no Neutral who seemed to enjoy the troubled times more than a woman called Jikonsahseh (Gi-gon-saw-say) "the Lynx." She had her lodge built on the main trail so she could watch the many war parties as they traveled across Neutral land. Jikonsahseh made her home available to the men, giving them not only shelter but food as well. She encouraged the fighters to eat as much as they desired from a large clay pot she kept full with meat some said was human flesh and sometimes poison. Afterwards she would fill their pipes with fresh tobacco, and while they were at ease she would ask them clever questions about their adventures.

Jikonsahseh was a collector of information which she used for power and profit. If a people wanted to know when their enemies would attack, they sent spies to Jikonsahseh laden with meat and furs. By the same token, if Jikonsahseh wished to destroy a village she could do so by giving its enemies information about its defenses, strengths, and weaknesses.

Jikonsahseh delighted in spreading gossip. She knew how to cause doubt and suspicion. Sometimes, for no other reason than her amusement, she would destroy

marriages and break apart families. She was as hated as she was feared, yet no one dared to move against her because she enjoyed the protection of powerful chiefs.

Such evil, although long endured, could not be carried on forever. One day Jikonsahseh heard rumors of a strange man wandering in Iroquois country. It seemed this man with white hair and light complexion was preaching a message of peace and calling for all nations to abandon warfare. Jikonsahseh was disturbed by this information and sent her allies far and wide to find this man. In time, she received news that he was coming from the east and would soon be at her lodge. Jikonsahseh trembled with doubt and fear. Soon she heard singing coming from over the hills and watched as a warm glow filled the eastern sky.

A man was walking towards her, his beautiful voice raised in a song so wonderful Jikonsahseh lost her fear and rose to welcome him into her home. Jikonsahseh looked closely at the man. He was young although his hair was of purest white. His speech was gentle, almost a whisper, and his words chosen with great care. He was clearly a man of dignity and grace. But it was his words, powerful and direct, which most affected Jikonsahseh.

He said he was sent by the Creator to bring people back to the path of peace. He was to form a world union of nations, all bound by a set of rules he called the Great Law of Peace. This divine message of goodness was to take root in the hearts of the most terrible peoples of all, the warring tribes of the Iroquois territories. He had entered the lands of the Mohawks after crossing Lake Ontario in a white stone canoe. Those who had heard his words called him the Peacemaker because he taught a different way of life which would end war. He had come to the territory of the Neutral Nation because he had heard of Jikonsahseh and wanted to persuade her to support his great plan.

Jikonsahseh was pleased that such a man would come to her. She saw the good in what he was saying. She had often wondered if there was a better way of living. Yes, she thought, her ways were indeed evil, but until now who had ever given her any hope life could be different? Jikonsahseh wept, for here finally was a glimmer of light in a dim and hostile world. She had been a bitter woman who trusted no one, but now she felt she could easily place her life in the hands of this gentle man.

Jikonsahseh listened to him for many days, forgetting thirst and hunger. She accepted as truth all of what he said. The Peacemaker went with her to the land of the Senecas, the fierce cousins of the bloody Mohawks. He brought her before the people, all of whom were surprised to see the despised Jikonsahseh in the company of the prophet.

The Peacemaker told the people Jikonsahseh had truly been a wicked woman but was now reborn into the ways of peace. Yet even in her acts of evil she had shown an intelligence upon which he would build his great league. She was the first human being to truly understand and accept with her whole heart the Great Law of Peace. Because of this the Peacemaker would give women the power to select and depose the leaders of their nations. They would be given the title of "clanmother." The people would choose clanmothers to direct the families while having the responsibility as lifegivers of deciding upon all matters relating to life.

Jikonsahseh was sent forth with the Peacemaker's message of hope. She settled among the Seneca Nation and there, in a town called Ganondagan, she persuaded the people to turn away from war and embrace peace.

Jikonsahseh was also present when the Great Tree of Peace was planted on the shores of Onondaga Lake marking the birth of the Haudenosaunee (Iroquois) Confederacy.

At Ganondagan she devoted the rest of her life to the teaching of the Great Law of Peace. So great was her wisdom, her council was sought by many Native peoples. She persuaded all who heard her to abandon warfare by following the Great Law. In her lifetime she was honored with the title Mother of Nations because she helped bring about a new and good way of living upon the earth.

Jikonsahseh is said to be buried at the state historical site known as Ganondagan, where thousands of people visit every year to hear about the origins of the Great Law of Peace. When she passed on to the spirit world, she left a tradition of strength and knowledge which is carried on by Iroquois women to this day.

DOUGLAS M. GEORGE-KANENTIIO is an award-winning freelance columnist for the *Syracuse Herald Journal* in Syracuse, New York, and a Native of the Akwesasne Mohawk Territory, Mohawk Nation. Nationally recognized as an authority on Iroquois politics and culture, he has served as advisor, producer, and script-writer for national television documentaries on Iroquois subjects.

JOANNE SHENANDOAH-TEKALIHWA: KHWA, a Wolf Clan member of Iroquois Confederacy, Oneida Nation, was selected 1994 Native Musician of the Year by the First Americans in the Arts Foundation, for preserving traditional values within the field of contemporary music. The winner of many other awards, she has made numerous recordings in the United States and abroad of music ranging from traditional chants to contemporary ballads about Native ways. Joanne Shenandoah resides in Oneida, New York with her husband, Douglas George, and their children.

JOHN KAHIONHES FADDEN is a renowned artist and illustrator, now retired from a long career in art education. His son DAVID KANIETAKERON FADDEN is a recognized artist in his own right. Both are members of the Mohawk Nation.